THE SOUND

KWAME ALEXANDER • ART BY CHARLY PALMER

LB
LITTLE, BROWN AND COMPANY
New York   Boston

For Alice, Percy, Richard, Gracie, and all the Johnsons,
who sang, danced, and laughed their way to love and happiness
most Saturday nights, and showed me how to do the same.
—KA

This book is for my beloved wife, Dr. Karida Brown,
and my enduring source of motivation, my mother, Irma Walker.
To my young family members, especially my wonderful children and grandchildren,
I dedicate this book with love and high hopes for your promising futures.
Lastly, I want to honor the memory of our joyful pug, Pugsley.
—CP

Listen to the fireside chorus
of the motherland
to the talking drums
dancing beneath the golden sun
that beat a bold tapestry
of yesterday's stories
and tomorrow's dreams.

To the magnetic chants that welcome each day
and the praise songs that sing us farewell.

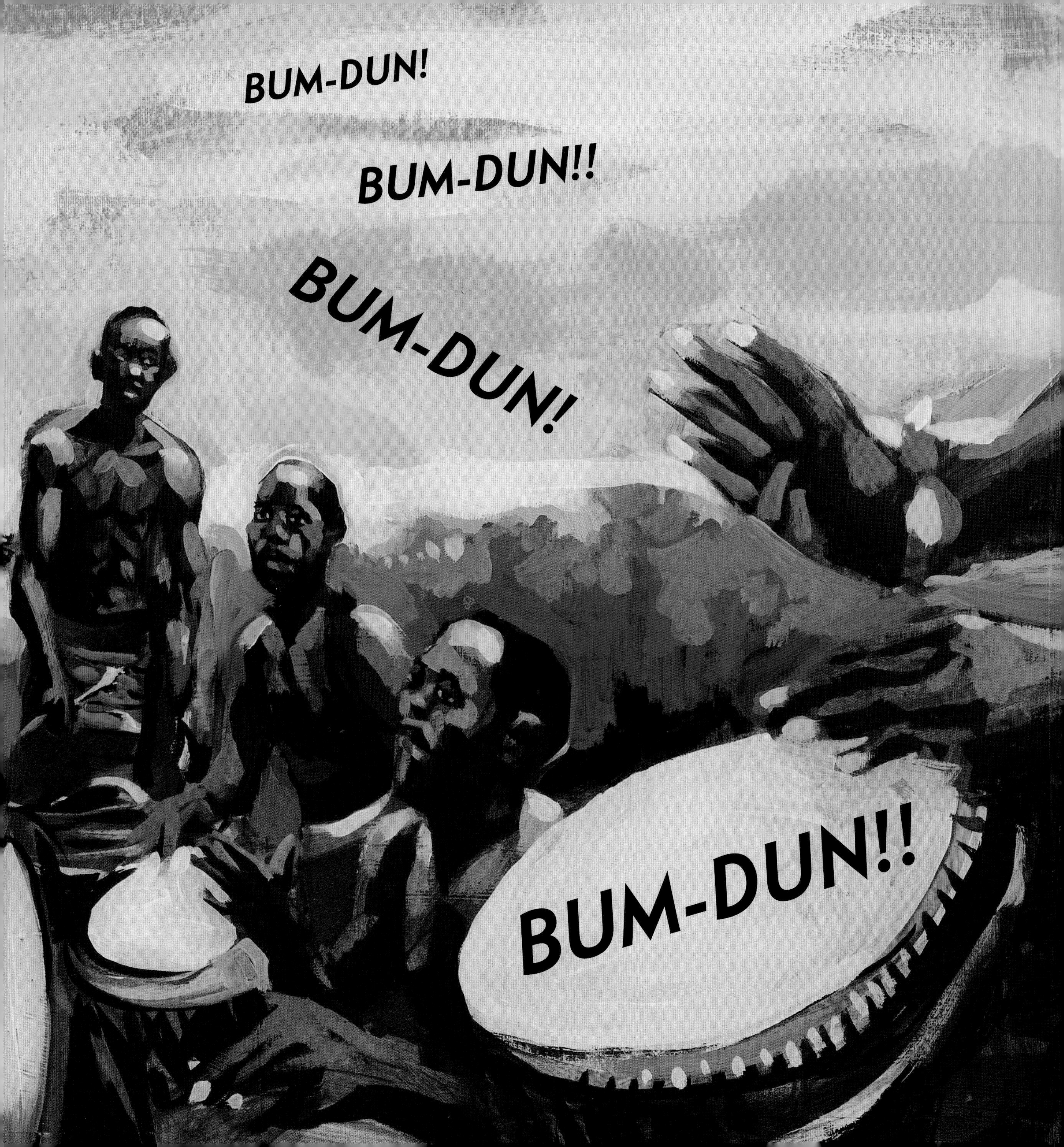
BUM-DUN!
BUM-DUN!!
BUM-DUN!
BUM-DUN!!

Listen to the hymns
that carried us away from home
across a blue unknown
to the faraway field hollers
that shouldered us
like sacks of summer cotton
from daybreak to sundown.

Listen to the work songs

JUBA JUBA JUBA!

and the Congo Square ring shouts
that telegraphed freedom
Soon and Very Soon.

Listen to the litanies that lifted
the insufferable weight off our world
to the spirituals that cleansed us
Under a Soprano Sky
Down by the Riverside
and filled us with everlasting hope
to the *Balm in Gilead*
and the psalms that healed us.

Listen to the *Amazing Grace*
of the Jubilee Singers
to the joyful noise
of Sunday morning gospel
and *Let the Church Say*

Listen to the deep blue-black moans
and the mellow croons
to the juke joint harmonicas
and the picnic banjos
to the brash Memphis blues
riding the rails
from the Mississippi Delta
all the way to the crossroads.

Yeah, listen to the simple melodies
that kept us laughing
to keep from crying
'cause *Nobody Knows You When You're Down*
and *if it wasn't for bad luck,*
I wouldn't have no luck at all.

Listen to the jazz.

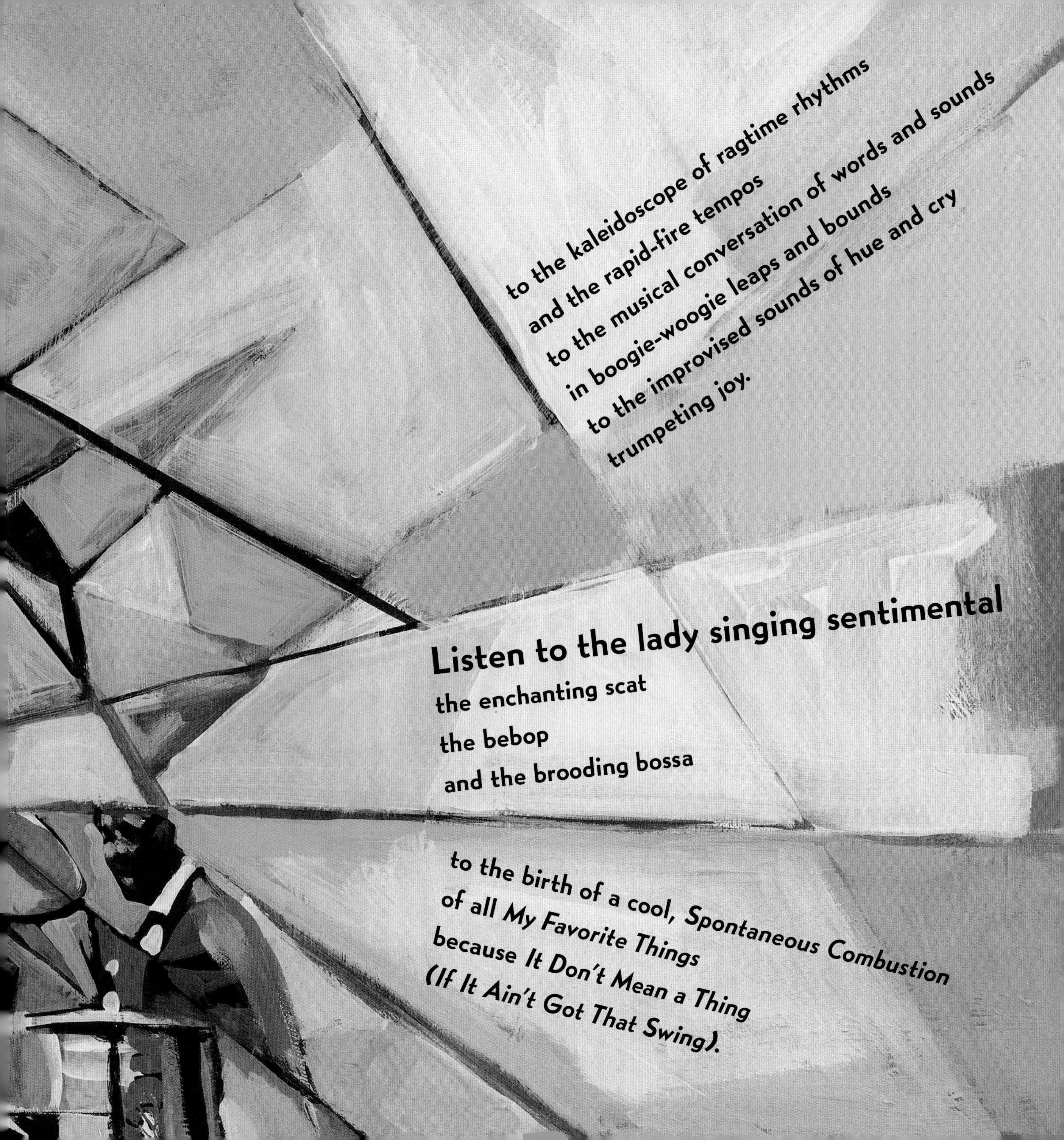

to the kaleidoscope of ragtime rhythms

and the rapid-fire tempos

to the musical conversation of words and sounds

in boogie-woogie leaps and bounds

to the improvised sounds of hue and cry

trumpeting joy.

Listen to the lady singing sentimental

the enchanting scat

the bebop

and the brooding bossa

to the birth of a cool, Spontaneous Combustion

of all My Favorite Things

because It Don't Mean a Thing

(If It Ain't Got That Swing).

Listen to the electric newness
of a revolution
to the lively and playful sounds
of youth shedding the shackles
of the Deep South
after the war
to the sonic innovators
and the flamboyant inventors
who rocked us around the clock
and had us dancing
into the *Wee Wee Hours*.
To the Duck Walk
and *The Twist*

to the star-spangled dignity
and the irresistible vibrations
from the steady drumbeats
hard-edged lyrics
and wailing vocals
of a booming generation of
unabashed rebels
asking themselves *What's Love Got to Do with It*
and screaming *Let's Go Crazy!*

Listen to the *Quiet Storm*
to the fast-paced rhythm of the *Street Life*
to the corner cries and croons
of freedom and love
of *Happy Feelin's*
that keep lifting you higher
because *Ain't Nothing Like the Real Thing.*

Listen to the music of the Godfather
and the Queen
of everything in *Between the Sheets*
to the medley
of the blues and the gospel
the jazz and the doo-wop
the stirring funk
that set souls on fire
and birthed a whole generation
that made us wanna holler
A Change Is Gonna Come
now *Say My Name*
and *Say It Loud,*
I'm Black and I'm Proud.

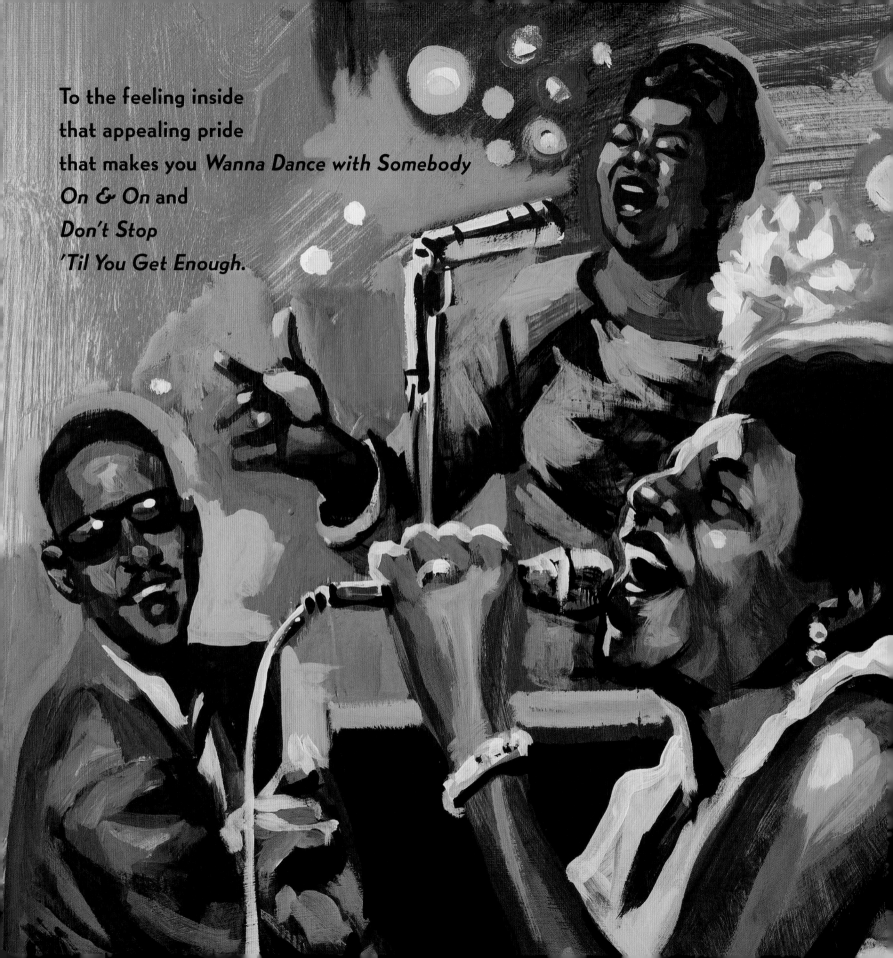

To the feeling inside
that appealing pride
that makes you *Wanna Dance with Somebody*
On & On and
Don't Stop
'Til You Get Enough.

Listen to *The Message*
from the Boogie Down Bronx
to the parties on the block
that made the planets rock
at *Tha Crossroads* of disco and drums.

To the soulful rhymes
break-dancing on concrete dreams
the tough-times poetry of the streets talking
the menacing beats walking
the way
of a new world
of a new sound
In da Club.

Yes, Yes, Y'all
to the *Good Times!*
To the *boom bap*
boom boom bap

boom **boom**
bap

boom
boom
bap.

To the grand masters
mixing and spinning
soft Black songs
sampling and flexing
their new jack swing
'til the break of dawn.

To the children's stories
and *The Playas' Anthems*
the low riders
and *The Big Steppers.*
To the tribe of stallions
making bold, beautiful jungle music
in this *Hard Knock Life.*
To the rhythm of our roots
that brought us, *Ready or Not,*
closer to freedom of mind
and fightin' the power
one Kool word at a time.

Yeah, listen
to all these sacred songs
and the many more.
To the reggae
and the rumba
to the country
and the folk
to the go-go
and the house.

To the hands clapping
and the feet sliding
to the kalimba
and the fiddle
to the wonder
and the woe.

Listen to the soundtrack of America
a symphony
of refuge and redemption
the sweet sound of a people
surviving and thriving
all the while learning
to love themselves
by singing it LOUD
and PROUD.

MUSICAL NOTES

Listen to the fireside chorus

talking drums: One of the oldest instruments from West Africa, the talking drums imitate the sound and cadence of language, enabling communication. During the enslavement of Africans in America, the drums were forbidden out of fear that they would be used to organize an uprising.

praise songs: Praise songs are a widely used African poetic form, recited orally and designed to describe and capture the essence or history of something or someone, especially a god, chief, or warrior.

Listen to the hymns

hymns: Hymns are songs of praise, devotion, celebration, or prayer. Drawing from their homeland music, Africans developed a rich tradition of singing religious hymns during times of slavery in America.

field hollers: Field hollers were work songs sung by enslaved African people. The songs, sung in the fields as the people performed backbreaking work under unspeakable conditions, created a connection among the people and were also used to communicate without the overseer knowing what was being said.

juba: With origins in Africa, juba is a percussive dance that includes complex, multilayered rhythms created by hand clapping, body slapping, and feet stomping. In the American South, enslaved people used juba not only as a dance, but as a replacement for the drums that had been taken from them. In the East African language of Swahili, juba means "work."

Congo Square: Congo Square was an open space in New Orleans where enslaved African people were permitted to gather. Over time, it became the center of music, dance, celebration, meetings, and eventually, the home of jazz. Today Congo Square is one corner of Louis Armstrong Park.

Soon and Very Soon: "Soon and Very Soon" is a well-known gospel hymn first written and performed by Andraé Crouch in 1976.

Listen to the litanies that lifted

litanies: Litanies are prayers or chants, most common in religious services. They are often repetitive in nature and use call and response, where someone recites a line and the congregation responds in unison.

spirituals: Spirituals are a type of religious hymn that grew out of the informal gatherings where enslaved African people in the American South danced, sang, and chanted. Centered on biblical stories and faith, spirituals convey sorrow and struggle as well as joy and hope.

Under a Soprano Sky: Published in 1987, *Under a Soprano Sky* is a collection of poetry by poet, activist, and scholar Sonia Sanchez. It includes a poem with the same title.

Down by the Riverside: Widely sung in churches today, "Down by the Riverside" was originally sung by enslaved African people working on plantations in the American South. A plantation melody with the same repeating phrase (although with a different title) was published by Black minister Marshall Taylor in his 1882 *Collection of Revival Hymns and Plantation Melodies*.

Balm in Gilead: The spiritual "Balm in Gilead" refers to healing the spirit and soul. It is based on scripture, in which the prophet Jeremiah was feeling depressed, his soul tortured. "Is there no balm in Gilead?" he asks, seeking solace. According to Black theologian Howard Thurman, enslaved people turned this question born of pain into a statement of optimism: "There is a balm in Gilead."

Amazing Grace: One of the most well-known Christian hymns, "Amazing Grace" was written in 1772 by English minister John Newton, a former slave trader. Newton had turned to religion in 1748, believing God had saved him during a storm at sea, but it wasn't until the mid-1780s that the Anglican minister became an abolitionist and openly challenged slavery. In 1835 in the United States, the words of "Amazing Grace" were paired with the hymn's now familiar tune.

Jubilee Singers: In 1871, Fisk University in Nashville sent its student choir on tour to raise money for the struggling school, which was founded to educate formerly enslaved people. The Black choir was called the Jubilee Singers because with emancipation the students had experienced a "year of jubilee," when scripture says all enslaved will be freed. The Jubilee Singers became renowned and performed at the White House in 1872. The next year the Jubilee Singers toured Great Britain and sang for Queen Victoria. The Fisk Jubilee Singers still perform today.

Let the Church Say Amen: "Let the Church Say Amen" is a gospel song first written and recorded by Andraé Crouch in 2011.

Listen to the deep blue-black moans

juke joint: Juke joints were places where Black people gathered to enjoy music and dance. In the Jim Crow South, they were safe spaces away from the threat of racism. Juke joints could be anywhere with a bar and stage area: shacks, open fields, even people's houses. They typically operated only when musicians were available, who often played only for tips.

Memphis blues: Blues is a genre of music created in the early 1900s by Black Americans in the rural South. Interweaving notes sung or played at a lower pitch, the blues expresses feelings of sadness, often due to hard times or struggles in love. Memphis was one of the Southern cities where Black Americans bought property and established businesses after the Civil War, making a thriving economic center that attracted musicians. In 1912, bandleader W. C. Handy published "The Memphis Blues," a campaign song he had written three years earlier during the Memphis mayoral race. Lacking the usual form, it was a blues song in name only, but Memphis became a hub for blues music in the **Mississippi Delta**.

crossroads: In some African cultures a crossroads is a mystical barrier guarded by a trickster that separates the human world from the divine. Such a crossroads is often associated with Delta bluesman Robert Johnson (1911–1938), whose mastery of the guitar was so great that people believed he must have met the devil himself at a crossroads and sold his soul to play so well. Johnson's songs "Cross Road Blues" and "Preachin' Blues (Up Jumped the Devil)" helped reinforce the myth. Johnson was inducted into the Rock and Roll Hall of Fame as an early influencer with its first class in 1986.

Nobody Knows You When You're Down: The song "Nobody Knows You When You're Down and Out" was recorded in 1929 by Bessie Smith (1894?–1937), one of the greatest blues singers of all time. She once toured with blues great Ma Rainey and spent years performing around the South before moving to Philadelphia, where in 1923 a representative of Columbia Records heard her sing and she began her recording career. Known for her rich con-

tralto voice and emotional intensity, Smith was inducted into the Blues Hall of Fame with its first class in 1980 and into the Rock and Roll Hall of Fame in 1989.

if it wasn't for bad luck, I wouldn't have no luck at all: These are lyrics from the song "Born Under a Bad Sign," first recorded in 1967 by Albert King (1923–1992), a blues musician whose unique style of guitar playing influenced generations of musicians, including Jimi Hendrix. Left-handed King played on a right-handed guitar turned upside down. King was inducted into the Blues Hall of Fame in 1983 and into the Rock and Roll Hall of Fame in 2013.

Listen to the jazz

jazz: Jazz is a wide-ranging genre of music with tempos, techniques, moods, and styles as varied as the musicians themselves. Jazz developed in the early 1900s in New Orleans, Louisiana; the first recordings date to 1917. Within jazz lives the history of Black people and Black music. A keystone of jazz is the improvisational solos, which spotlight individuality, creativity, and excellence. Among the pioneers of jazz are Louis Armstrong, Duke Ellington, Miles Davis, and Charlie Parker. Many consider jazz to be America's classical music and its greatest artistic contribution to the world.

to the kaleidoscope of ragtime rhythms

ragtime: A forerunner of jazz, ragtime is an American genre of syncopated piano music that rose to great popularity in the early 1900s. Pianist and composer Scott Joplin was considered the king of ragtime. Two of his famous songs were "Maple Leaf Rag" from 1899 and "The Entertainer" from 1902, which hit the pop charts in 1974 after it was used in the movie *The Sting*.

boogie-woogie: Boogie-woogie is a rugged, percussive style of blues piano music, where the right hand plays riffs against a driving bass played by the left. Usually played fast, boogie-woogie became popular in the urban centers of Chicago, Detroit, and New York in the 1920s. The man considered to be the greatest boogie-woogie pianist, Jimmy Yancey, played piano only as a sideline to his job as groundskeeper for the Chicago White Sox, but his style was so influential that he was inducted into the inaugural class of the Rock and Roll Hall of Fame, in 1986.

improvised sounds: With his energetic solos, trumpeter Louis Armstrong (1901–1971) was one of the most influential figures in jazz. He was known for his gravelly voice and improvisational singing as well as his wide smile **trumpeting joy** wherever he performed. His career as a musician, bandleader, composer, and sometime actor spanned the 1920s through the 1960s, and in 2017, he was inducted into the Rhythm & Blues Hall of Fame.

lady singing sentimental: In 1956, vocalist Billie Holiday (1915–1959) released an album titled *Lady Sings the Blues*, which included a song of the same name. Billie Holiday was one of America's greatest jazz singers, known for her raspy voice and dramatic intensity. Several of her recordings have been inducted into the Grammy Hall of Fame for their lasting quality or historical significance, including "Strange Fruit" from 1939 and "God Bless the Child" from 1941.

enchanting scat: Scat is a style of singing in which vocalists use nonsense syllables to improvise the sound of an instrument. Along with Louis Armstrong, one of the best singers of scat was Ella Fitzgerald (1917–1996), the First Lady of Song and the Queen of Jazz. Fitzgerald had a gift for phrasing and could sing anything from ballads to bebop. She collaborated with many jazz artists, including Louis Armstrong and Duke Ellington. In 2000 a compilation of her radio performances was called *The Enchanting Ella Fitzgerald*.

bebop: Bebop evolved in the mid-1940s as a more modern form of jazz. Earlier jazz consisted of melodies and harmonies based on major and minor seven-note scales. But bebop used all twelve notes of the chromatic scale and added chords and complicated double-time rhythms to the traditional harmonies, creating complex improvisations. Musicians Charlie Parker, Dizzy Gillespie, Charlie Christian, Thelonious Monk, and Kenny Clarke are credited with the origination of bebop.

bossa: Bossa nova, which means "new trend" in Portuguese, is a Brazilian style of music that blends a smooth samba rhythm with cool jazz, a slower, more subdued form of jazz. It uses a classical guitar with one or two other instruments, allowing a singer room to improvise. Created in the 1950s by Antônio Carlos Jobim and guitarist João Gilberto, bossa nova spread to the United States in the 1960s.

birth of a cool: In 1957, the landmark album by Miles Davis (1926–1991), *Birth of the Cool*, was released. Miles Davis was a jazz trumpeter, bandleader, and composer. He is one of the most influential and acclaimed figures in jazz and twentieth-century music, inspiring musicians across many genres. Throughout his fifty-year career, his innovations helped shape the course of music. In 1948, he added the traditionally classical French horn to his band.

While most jazz at the time contained complicated rhythms, his style was melodic, relaxed, and mellow. Miles Davis was inducted into the Rock and Roll Hall of Fame in 2006.

Spontaneous Combustion: "Spontaneous Combustion" is a 1955 recording by jazz saxophonist Cannonball Adderley (1928–1975). Adderley, whose given name was Julian, played alongside John Coltrane in Miles Davis's group and was one of the most prominent jazz musicians of the 1950s and 1960s. Adderley's straightforward, exuberant music appealed to the mainstream and helped keep jazz popular as it began to move in a more complex direction.

My Favorite Things: Written by Richard Rodgers and Oscar Hammerstein, "My Favorite Things" was recorded as a jazz instrumental in 1960 by John Coltrane (1926–1967), one of the great jazz saxophonists. Coltrane first came to prominence in 1955, when he joined Miles Davis's quintet. He was known for his intense, powerful style, pouring a cascade of notes out of his saxophone during his improvisational solos.

It Don't Mean a Thing (If It Ain't Got That Swing): "It Don't Mean a Thing (If It Ain't Got That Swing)" is a jazz song written by Duke Ellington (1899–1974), one of America's greatest composers. Ellington wrote more than two thousand songs, mostly for the jazz orchestra he led for nearly half a century. This song, written with Irving Mills, epitomized the swing style of jazz played by big bands in the 1930s and 1940s.

Listen to the electric newness

sonic innovators and **flamboyant inventors:** Among the innovators who put rock and roll on the map were renowned Black musicians. Jazz guitarist Charlie Christian in 1936 was one of the first to improvise using electrically amplified equipment, bringing the guitar to the forefront. Switching to an electric Gibson in 1947, Sister Rosetta Tharpe became the first gospel rock star and the godmother of rock and roll. Electric guitarist Chuck Berry brought us not only rock and roll songs such as "Wee Wee Hours" but also his flamboyant **Duck Walk**.

The Twist: "The Twist" was originally a rhythm and blues song released in 1959 by Hank Ballard and the Midnighters. Dick Clark, the producer of *American Bandstand*, learned that kids in Baltimore were dancing to it and suggested it be re-recorded for a mainstream audience. Teenager Ernest Evans, stage name Chubby Checker, was enlisted to make a cover, and on the evening of August 6, 1960, he performed "The Twist" with his own dance moves on ABC's *Dick Clark Show*, sparking a national craze.

to the wop bop a loo bop

wop bop a loo bop and **lop bom bom:** These are lyrics from the song "Tutti Frutti" by Little Richard (1932-2020). Born Richard Wayne Penniman, Little Richard was a trailblazing singer, piano player, and rock and roll pioneer. He grew up singing gospel and left home as a teenager to play rhythm and blues in clubs, where he became known for his high-energy antics onstage. In 1955 and 1956, he recorded "Tutti Frutti" and a string of other hits for Specialty Records. Like many Black artists back then, Little Richard signed a highly exploitative contract with the label, which had bought the publishing rights to "Tutti Frutti" for $50. While white performers were getting three to five cents for each record sold, Little Richard received only half a cent. By the time "Tutti Frutti" had sold five hundred thousand copies, he had only earned $25,000. By 1968, over three million copies had sold. In 1984, Little Richard sued Specialty Records and settled for an undisclosed amount. Little Richard was one of the original inductees into the Rock and Roll Hall of Fame, in 1986.

star-spangled dignity: Guitarist Jimi Hendrix (1942-1970) famously played "The Star-Spangled Banner" on the last day of Woodstock in 1969. A self-taught guitarist who couldn't read music, Hendrix revolutionized rock and roll in the 1960s with his technique, showmanship, and experimental use of music technology to create distortion and psychedelic effects. In 1967 his band, the Jimi Hendrix Experience, was one of the highest-paid touring bands in the world. The Jimi Hendrix Experience was inducted into the Rock and Roll Hall of Fame in 1992.

What's Love Got to Do with It: "What's Love Got to Do with It" is a Grammy-winning single off the first rock album by Tina Turner (1939-2023). Born Anna Mae Bullock, Turner joined Ike Turner's rhythm and blues band as a vocalist while still a teenager in high school in St. Louis. In the 1960s they skyrocketed to fame as R&B artists together. As a solo artist in 1984, Tina Turner released her first rock album, *Private Dancer*, which sold over twenty million copies and won three Grammys. She was inducted into the Rock and Roll Hall of Fame in 2021.

Let's Go Crazy: "Let's Go Crazy" is a single off the 1984 album *Purple Rain* by Prince (1958-2016). Prince Rogers Nelson was a singer, songwriter, dancer, producer, and musician, often playing every instrument on his albums himself. His music crossed genres, with notes of jazz, rock and roll, R&B, and funk. Arguably the most talented, innovative performer of his generation, Prince advocated for both creative and financial freedom and broke free of the traditional music industry, changing his name at one point to an unpronounceable symbol and controlling all aspects of his creative life. He occasionally acted in films, including the movie *Purple Rain*, whose music earned him an Oscar and a Grammy. In 2004, Prince was inducted into the Rock and Roll Hall of Fame.

Listen to the Quiet Storm

Quiet Storm: In 1975, singer Smokey Robinson released an album titled *A Quiet Storm*, which had a smooth vibe. The next year station manager Cathy Hughes at Howard University's WHUR in Washington, DC, used the album's title track as the theme for a nightly show of slow jams—slow songs with influences of rhythm and blues, soul, and jazz. Radio stations around the country copied the show's format and its theme, leading to the radio format called quiet storm.

rhythm: Rhythm and blues officially became a music genre in 1949 when future record producer Jerry Wexler, working at *Billboard* at the time, suggested "rhythm and blues" as a replacement for "race records" on the magazine's weekly sales chart for Black music. Originating in the 1940s, traditional R&B combines elements of pop, gospel, blues, and jazz with a strong backbeat. Although R&B grew in tandem with rock and roll in the 1950s, the genres diverged in the 1960s as crooning vocalists smoothed out the R&B sound. In the 1970s, artists brought expanded instrumentation and African rhythms into the R&B mix.

Street Life: "Street Life" is the title track of a smooth-jazz album released by the Crusaders in 1979.

Happy Feelin's: "Happy Feelin's" is a funk song off the first album released by the R&B group Maze featuring Frankie Beverly in 1977. Evolved from R&B, funk is a type of dance music with a syncopated bass style and a steady drumbeat.

Ain't Nothing Like the Real Thing: "Ain't Nothing Like the Real Thing" is a duet by Marvin Gaye and Tammi Terrell released by Motown Records in 1968. Founded in 1959 by Berry Gordy in Detroit, Michigan, Motown was one of the most successful Black-owned businesses in US history and one of the most influential independent record labels.

Listen to the music of the Godfather

Godfather and **Queen:** James Brown was the Godfather of Soul and Aretha Franklin, the Queen. Soul music grew out of rhythm and blues, the main difference being expression. Soul artists often sang with such intense emotion that they seemed possessed. In some ways soul represented a return to two roots of Black music, gospel and blues. Both Brown and Franklin started out as gospel singers. Soul songs are sung with passion, whether they are about love and relationships—like the Isley Brothers' **"Between the Sheets"** from 1983 and **"Say My Name"** by Destiny's Child from 1999—or about social justice—like Marvin Gaye's **"Inner City Blues (Make Me Wanna Holler)"** from 1971 and Sam Cooke's **"A Change Is Gonna Come"** from 1964. James Brown's 1969 song **"Say It Loud, I'm Black and I'm Proud"** became a mantra for the Black community.

To the feeling inside

Wanna Dance with Somebody: "I Wanna Dance with Somebody (Who Loves Me)" is a Grammy-winning pop single recorded in 1987 by Whitney Houston (1963-2012). Singing since she was a child in church, Houston released a self-titled debut album in 1985 that produced three number one singles, a first for a female artist. Houston was inducted into the Rock and Roll Hall of Fame in 2020.

On & On: "On & On," from 1997, is the Grammy-winning debut single of Erykah Badu. Along with artists Angie Stone and Jill Scott, Badu is credited with developing Neo Soul. Coined by Motown executive Kedar Massenburg, Neo Soul describes music that has smooth vocals and catchy melodies like classic soul but also incorporates hip-hop, funk, and rock beats. Songs often combine live and sampled music and feature electronic beats.

Don't Stop 'Til You Get Enough: "Don't Stop 'Til You Get Enough" from 1979 is one of seventeen number one hits sung by Michael Jackson (1958-2009) in a musical career that spanned nearly his entire life. Beginning at age five, he performed with his siblings as lead singer of the Jackson 5 and went on to build a solo career as an adult, becoming the King of Pop. He was inducted into the Rock and Roll Hall of Fame in 2001.

Listen to The Message

The Message: Released by Grandmaster Flash and the Furious Five, "The Message" is an early influential rap song from 1982. Rap came out of the hip-hop culture that originated in the **Bronx** in the 1970s. Star DJs spun soul and R&B records at parties and dance clubs, while MCs pumped up the crowd. As the culture evolved, MCs came to the forefront, speaking in rhymes, or rapping, over the DJs' music. "The Message," with its bleak imagery of life in the ghetto, helped push rap away from good-time party lyrics into more direct social commentary. The song's synthesizer and rhythm tracks have since been sampled in hip-hop songs hundreds of times.

Tha Crossroads and **In da Club:** These are two of hip-hop's biggest-selling songs. "Tha Crossroads," by Bone Thugs-N-Harmony, spent eight weeks on *Billboard*'s Hot 100 chart in 1996. "In Da Club," by rapper 50 Cent, spent nine weeks at number one in 2003.

break-dancing: Break-dancing is one of the four pillars of hip-hop culture, along with DJing, MCing (rapping), and graffiti. Break-dancers perform energetic, acrobatic moves to the percussion breaks created by DJs sampling different records.

Yes, Yes, Y'all

Yes, Yes, Y'all: This was a popular chant of affirmation at parties hosted by DJs known as **grand masters.** Grand masters kept parties going by sampling tracks and mixing songs from different records. Using more than one turntable, the DJs overlapped songs and "scratched" by disrupting the rotation of the record to create additional rhythms from dance tunes like Chic's **"Good Times"** from 1979.

boom bap: An onomatopoeia prominently used in hip-hop, it represents the sound of the bass drum and the snare drum, respectively.

new jack swing: A subgenre of R&B pioneered by Teddy Riley in the 1980s, new jack swing was an upbeat, fast-paced blend of hip-hop, soul, and pop, characterized by sharp beats and meaty bass lines topped with a mixture of rapping and soulful singing.

To the children's stories

children's stories: "Children's Story" was recorded by rapper Slick Rick in 1989.

The Playas' Anthems: Hip-hop artists OutKast and UGK recorded "Int'l Players Anthem (I Choose You)" together in 2007.

The Big Steppers: Rapper Kendrick Lamar came out with his seventh album, *Mr. Morale & The Big Steppers*, in 2022.

stallions: Megan Thee Stallion, a rapper from Houston, won the Grammy for Best New Artist in 2021.

Hard Knock Life: *Hard Knock Life*, from 1998, is the title of Jay-Z's second album.

Ready or Not: Lauryn Hill recorded "Ready or Not" in 1996 as a member of the hip-hop group the Fugees.

fightin' the power: Public Enemy recorded the rap classic "Fight the Power" in 1989 for Spike Lee's movie *Do the Right Thing*.

Kool: Clive Campbell (1955–), a Jamaican-born DJ known as Kool Herc, is widely celebrated as the originator of hip-hop with his innovations on the turntables as a party DJ in the Bronx in 1973.

Yeah, listen

reggae: Derived from the Jamaican term *rege*, meaning "ragged," reggae originated in poor areas of Kingston, Jamaica, in the 1960s. It evolved from ska, an urban Jamaican music that developed from imported New Orleans rhythm and blues recordings in the 1950s. Reggae uses a heavy four-beat rhythm, defined by electric bass, guitar, and drums. Because of its social and political commentary, reggae is often regarded as the voice of an oppressed people. Reggae has blended into other genres, and its influence on today's music is widespread.

rumba: Rumba grew out of the dances of enslaved Congolese people in Cuba, emerging from the island's impoverished Black areas in the late 1800s. Traditional rumba involves rhythmic dancing to percussive music played on conga drums and tapped sticks, along with a lead singer performing call and response with a chorus. As the music spread internationally in the twentieth century, rumba became a catchall term for all Afro-Cuban music, including son, a style that combines African rhythms with Spanish guitars. Today rumba is also a ballroom dance.

country: Country music is a complex genre born of American rural life. Its roots date back to the 1600s, when Europeans arrived with their fiddles and centuries-old folk ballads, bringing along enslaved African people, who fashioned the first banjos out of gourds in an effort to re-create their traditional stringed instruments. Over time, white fiddle music and Black banjo music formed the basis of country music. The advent of recorded music and radio in the early twentieth century increased the popularity and scope of the genre, as country artists incorporated elements of gospel, blues, jazz, and later, rock and roll into their music.

folk: Folk music is traditional music that is passed down orally through families and small communities from generation to generation. Performed by amateurs, traditional folk is the music of annual rituals and daily life, with style and meaning varying from community to community and era to era. Guitars, banjos, and fiddles are commonly used. In the middle of the twentieth century, professional artists brought folk music into popular culture, associating it with the civil rights movement, environmental politics, and antiwar protests.

go-go: Go-go originated in Washington, DC, in the mid- to late 1970s. Chuck Brown and his band the Soul Searchers laid the foundation for this relaxed style of funk, which incorporated call-and-response chants and Afro-Caribbean rhythms and instruments, and was often performed nonstop to keep people on the dance floor.

house: In the early 1980s, Black DJs in Chicago pioneered house music, an electronic high-tempo dance music influenced by soul and disco, the preeminent dance music of the 1970s. House music is known for its steady kick-drum beat in four-four time, the use of synthesizers and drum machines, and a fast pace of 120 to 130 beats per minute. The origin of the name is unclear. Some believe it came from a place called "The Warehouse" where the music was played, while others think it's because house music allowed DJs to produce the music at home rather than in an expensive studio. House music spread quickly to cities across America and Europe.

kalimba: The kalimba is a modern adaption of the mbira, an African instrument with a wooden soundboard and metal keys that are played by depressing and releasing them with the thumbs and fingers.